# Asian Animals

# Komodo Dragons

ABDO
Publishing Company

Big Buddy BOOKS
Asian Animals

by Julie Murray

Published by ABDO Publishing Company, PO Box 398166, Minneapolis, Minnesota 55439.

Printed in the United States of America, North Mankato, Minnesota.
102012
012013

 PRINTED ON RECYCLED PAPER

Coordinating Series Editor: Rochelle Baltzer
Editor: Marcia Zappa
Contributing Editors: Grace Hansen, Stephanie Hedlund, Sarah Tieck
Graphic Design: Maria Hosley
Cover Photograph: *Fotosearch.com*.
Interior Photographs/Illustrations: *Fotosearch.com*: ©vulkanette (p. 21); *Glow Images*: Wolfgang Kaehler/Superstock (p. 23); *iStockphoto*: ©iStockphoto.com/HU-JUN (p. 4), ©iStockphoto.com/maksfoto (p. 5); *Minden Pictures*: Michael Pitts/npl (pp. 25, 27); *National Geographic Stock*: MAURICIO HANDLER (p. 23), MICHAEL NICHOLS (p. 15); *Rodmorris.co.nz* (p. 15); *Shutterstock*: Warren Goldswain (p. 9), Image Focus (p. 4), Khoroshunova Olga (p. 9), Pius Lee (pp. 11, 19), Nathape (p. 13), Uryadnikov Sergey (pp. 7, 17, 19, 29), Takashi Usui (p. 8), Worldpics (p. 9).

### Library of Congress Cataloging-in-Publication Data

Murray, Julie, 1969-
    Komodo dragons / Julie Murray.
        p. cm. -- (Asian animals)
    Audience: 7-11
    ISBN 978-1-61783-555-1
    1. Komodo dragon--Asia--Juvenile literature.  I. Title.
    QL666.L29M87 2013
    597.95'968--dc23
                                    2012030859

# Contents

Amazing Asian Animals . . . . . . . . . . . . . . . . . . . . . . . . . 4

Komodo Dragon Territory . . . . . . . . . . . . . . . . . . . . . . .6

Welcome to Asia! . . . . . . . . . . . . . . . . . . . . . . . . . . . .8

Take a Closer Look . . . . . . . . . . . . . . . . . . . . . . . . . 10

Independent Life . . . . . . . . . . . . . . . . . . . . . . . . . 14

Mighty Hungry . . . . . . . . . . . . . . . . . . . . . . . . . . 16

Great Hunters . . . . . . . . . . . . . . . . . . . . . . . . . . 18

Mealtime . . . . . . . . . . . . . . . . . . . . . . . . . . . . . 22

Incredible Eggs . . . . . . . . . . . . . . . . . . . . . . . . . 24

Baby Dragons . . . . . . . . . . . . . . . . . . . . . . . . . . 26

Survivors . . . . . . . . . . . . . . . . . . . . . . . . . . . . . 28

Wow! I'll bet you never knew... . . . . . . . . . . . . . . . . . 30

Important Words . . . . . . . . . . . . . . . . . . . . . . . . . 31

Web Sites . . . . . . . . . . . . . . . . . . . . . . . . . . . . . 31

Index . . . . . . . . . . . . . . . . . . . . . . . . . . . . . . . 32

Long ago, nearly all land on Earth was one big mass. About 200 million years ago, the land began to break into **continents**. One of these continents is Asia.

4

The Komodo dragon is the largest living lizard on Earth!

Asia is the largest **continent**. It includes many countries and **cultures**. It also has different types of land and interesting animals. One of these animals is the Komodo dragon. In the wild, they are only found in Asia.

# Komodo Dragon Territory

Komodo dragons live on islands in the Southeast Asian country of Indonesia. These include Komodo, Rinca, Flores, and several smaller islands.

Komodo dragons usually live in hot, dry grasslands and forests. But, they can also be found on beaches and cliffs.

 Komodo Dragon Territory

The islands Komodo dragons live on are very small. Komodo is the largest island, at only 22 miles (35 km) long!

# Welcome to Asia!

If you took a trip to where Komodo dragons live, you might find…

## …water.

Bodies of water surround the Komodo dragon's island territory. They are home to more than 1,000 types of fish! They are also home to whales, dolphins, and sea turtles.

## ...wild land.

Hundreds of Komodo dragons live in Komodo National Park. The Indonesian government set aside this land to protect them and their habitat. The park includes several islands and the water surrounding them. In all, it is more than 700 square miles (1,800 sq km).

## ...rice.

Indonesia is one of the world's leading rice growers. It has many mountains. So, rice is often grown on large steps called terraces.

## ...many people.

Indonesia is the fourth most-populated country in the world! Only China, India, and the United States have more people. Most of Indonesia's people live on the country's larger islands, such as Java. Java is home to Jakarta (*right*), Indonesia's largest city.

9

# Take a Closer Look

Adult Komodo dragons have thick bodies and large, strong tails. Their short, thick legs are bowed. These animals have long necks. They have flat heads with rounded **snouts**.

A Komodo dragon's body is covered in scales. Adults are brown, gray, or dull red in color.

Komodo dragons have long, yellow tongues that are split at the end. Many people believe this makes them look like fire-breathing dragons. That is how the Komodo dragon got its name.

Adult male Komodo dragons grow up to ten feet (3 m) long. And, they generally weigh 150 to 300 pounds (68 to 136 kg). Males are slightly larger than females.

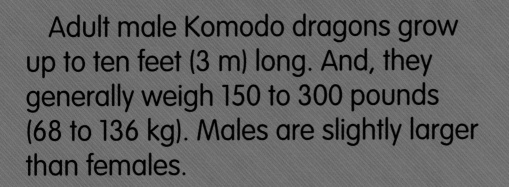

**Uncovered!**
The largest Komodo dragon ever measured was 10.3 feet (3.1 m) long and 366 pounds (166 kg). But, a lot of this weight was probably from food in its belly.

There are four times as many wild male Komodo dragons as there are females.

# Independent Life

Komodo dragons generally live alone. They stay in certain home areas. But, their home areas include shared land. And, they come together to feed.

Male Komodo dragons often fight to prove who is most powerful. The dragon that wins gets to eat first. Male dragons also fight for the chance to **mate** with females.

**Uncovered!**
A Komodo dragon's home area is about one square mile (3 sq km).

14

Komodo dragons dig underground homes called burrows. They sleep in these at night and during the hottest part of the day.

Komodo dragons fight by standing on their back legs. Then, they battle with their front feet. They use their powerful tails for support.

# Mighty Hungry

Komodo dragons are **carnivores**. They often eat animals that are already dead. But, they also hunt live **prey**. This includes deer, goats, pigs, water buffalo, and smaller Komodo dragons.

A Komodo dragon can eat 80 percent of its body weight in one meal!

Komodo dragons eat almost any kind of meat they can find. They have even been known to eat humans!

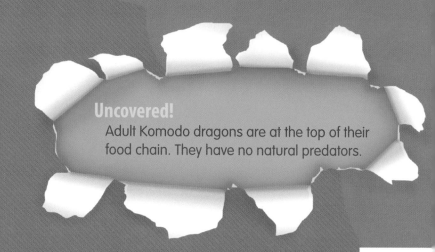

**Uncovered!**
Adult Komodo dragons are at the top of their food chain. They have no natural predators.

# Great Hunters

Komodo dragons hunt alone. Usually, a dragon hides and waits for its **prey**. Then, it springs at it. A dragon uses its strong legs, sharp claws, and teeth to kill its prey.

Sometimes, Komodo dragons spend hours in one spot waiting for prey.

Komodo dragons can run faster than ten miles (16 km) per hour for a short length. This helps them catch some small prey.

A Komodo dragon may not be able to kill its **prey** right away. But, its bite is full of **venom**. So, a dragon's bitten prey will usually die within a week.

Sometimes, a Komodo dragon slowly follows its bitten prey. The dragon waits for it to die. Other times, it gives up and other dragons later eat the dead prey.

**Uncovered!**
A Komodo dragon's venom is not deadly to other dragons.

Komodo dragons use the tips of their tongues to smell. They are able to smell a meal several miles away! They also use their vision and hearing to hunt prey.

# Mealtime

Komodo dragons eat large amounts of food very quickly. They have stretchy throats and a mouth that opens extra wide. This allows them to swallow large chunks of meat. Komodo dragons waste little of their prey. They eat bones, hooves, skin, and insides.

Komodo dragons have about 60 small teeth. They are curved and jagged like saws. A dragon goes through four or five sets of teeth during its life!

Komodo dragons often eat together in a group. The most powerful males eat first. Then, smaller males and females eat.

# Incredible Eggs

Komodo dragons are reptiles. They are born from eggs. First, a female dragon digs a shallow nest in the ground. Then, she lays 15 to 30 eggs in the nest. She covers the eggs with leaves and dirt.

A female Komodo dragon usually stays with her eggs. She guards them and keeps them warm. She waits until they are ready to hatch.

Komodo dragon eggs have soft, white shells.

**Uncovered!**
Female Komodo dragons usually lay their eggs in September. They wait until after the hot, dry summer months.

# Baby Dragons

Komodo dragon babies **hatch** after seven to nine months. Newly hatched dragons are 12 to 24 inches (30 to 61 cm) long. They weigh about 3.5 ounces (99.2 g).

Adult Komodo dragons do not take care of their babies. Babies climb into trees to stay safe from predators, including adult dragons.

Young Komodo dragons stay in trees. There, they eat bugs, eggs, and small lizards, snakes, and birds. After several months, they are big enough to live on the ground.

Young Komodo dragons have colorful markings. They can be green, yellow, brown, gray, or black. Their scales change color as they grow.

**Uncovered!**
Adult Komodo dragons are too heavy to climb trees.

**Uncovered!**
Komodo dragons are vulnerable. This means they are in some danger of dying out.

# Survivors

Life in Asia isn't easy for Komodo dragons. New buildings and farms take over their **habitat**. **Prey** is not as common as it once was. And, some people kill Komodo dragons.

Still, Komodo dragons **survive**. There are laws in Indonesia against killing them. And, people are working to save their habitat. Komodo dragons help make Asia an amazing place!

In the wild, Komodo dragons live for 20 to 50 years.

# Wow!
## I'll bet you never knew...

...that Komodo dragons have lived in Asia for millions of years. But, the islands they live on are very small and have few people. So, scientists did not know the dragons existed until about 100 years ago!

...that a Komodo dragon's bite is weaker than a house cat's! But, a dragon's extra-sharp teeth and **venom** make its bite deadly.

...that one local name for Komodo dragons is *buaja darat*. It means "land crocodile."

...that Komodo dragons are good swimmers. They enjoy cooling off in the water. And, they have been known to swim between islands.

# Important Words

**carnivore** (KAHR-nuh-vawr) an animal or a plant that eats meat.

**continent** one of Earth's seven main land areas.

**culture** (KUHL-chuhr) the arts, beliefs, and ways of life of a group of people.

**habitat** a place where a living thing is naturally found.

**hatch** to be born from an egg.

**mate** to join as a couple in order to reproduce, or have babies.

**prey** an animal hunted or killed by a predator for food.

**reptile** a member of a group of living beings. Reptiles have scaly skin and are cold-blooded.

**snout** a part of the face, including the nose and the mouth, that sticks out. Some animals, such as Komodo dragons, have a snout.

**survive** to continue to live or exist.

**venom** a poison made by some animals and insects. It usually enters a victim through a bite or a sting.

# Web Sites

To learn more about Komodo dragons, visit ABDO Publishing Company online. Web sites about Komodo dragons are featured on our Book Links page. These links are routinely monitored and updated to provide the most current information available.

## www.abdopublishing.com

# Index

Asia **4, 5, 6, 28, 30**

body **10, 15, 18, 22**

burrows **15**

dangers **26, 28**

eating habits **14, 16, 17, 20, 22, 23, 26**

eggs **24, 25**

fighting **14, 15**

Flores **6**

habitat **6, 9, 28**

hunting **16, 18, 19, 20, 21**

Indonesia **6, 9, 28**

Komodo **6, 7**

Komodo National Park **9**

mating **14**

reptiles **24**

Rinca **6**

scales **10, 27**

size **5, 12, 26**

teeth **18, 23, 30**

tongues **11, 21**

venom **20, 30**

weather **6, 15, 25**

young Komodo dragons **26, 27**